THE KAFKA SUTRA

Robert Archambeau

MadHat Press
Asheville, North Carolina

MadHat Press
MadHat Incorporated
PO Box 8364, Asheville, NC 28814

The Library of Congress has assigned
this edition a Control Number of
2015913495

ISBN 978-1-941196-20-5 (paperback)

Text by Robert Archambeau
Cover photograph by Kris Abgail
Book and cover design by MadHat Press

www.MadHat-Press.com

First Printing

THE KAFKA SUTRA

For Jean-Luc, *mon vieux*

CONTENTS

ACKNOWLEDGEMENTS

Many of these poems have appeared in other publications: From "The Kafka Sutra," the pieces "Introductory," "The Great Wall and the Tower of Babel," "An Imperial Message," "Couriers," "Before the Door," and "Parables" appeared in *The Cultural Society*, as did "Sheena is a Punk Rocker," "Manifest Destinies, Black Rains" and "Nag Hammadi: A Parable," which also appeared in the anthology *New Poetry from the Midwest*. Other pieces from "The Kafka Sutra" ("Leopards in the Temple" and "The Ball Rider") appeared in *The Laurel Review*. "English Majors" appeared in *Fulcrum*, "Lecture Hall" and "Cooking Without Milton" were published in *Cimarron Review*, "Hieratic Perspective" and "Working the Piano" (as "For John Matthias") appeared in *The Battersea Review*, "Letter to Albert Goldbarth" and "Brightness Falls" were published in *P.F.S. Post*, "The Poem that Does Not Exist" was featured in the anthology *Litscapes*. "A Note on the Poetry of Lucie Thésée," "Sarabande" and "Poem ('Handsome …')" appeared in *Poetry*, as did "A Pedal-Pusher Said to Me," while "Poem ('My Head')" and "Rapture: The Depths" appeared in *Circumference*. "Hierarchy: A Night" appeared in *Action Yes!* and was featured on BBC Radio 3. The afterword to this book, "Hating the Other Kind of Poetry," appeared in slightly different form in *Copper Nickel*.

Many of the free and loose versions (one hesitates to call them translations) that appear in part four of this book are the products of back-and-forth dialogue with Jean-Luc Garneau. The images that accompany "The Kafka Sutra" were made by the artist Sarah Conner, and shown at the Chicago Printmaker's Collaborative. I am grateful to Jean-Luc and to Sarah for their friendship, generosity, and collaboration.

The cover image, featuring the model Moxie, appears courtesy of photographer Kris Abigail.

I

THE KAFKA SUTRA

Source texts: Kafka's parables and the *Kama Sutra*.

Images by Sarah Conner.

INTRODUCTORY

In the beginning the Lord of Lords created men and women, and in the form of commandments in one hundred thousand chapters laid down rules for the proper governance of the Dharma, Artha, and Kama. Those rules which treated of Dharma were disclosed by Swayambhu Manu; those governing Artha were compiled by Brihaspati; and those that referred to Kama were, such is the mystery of mysteries, expounded by Franz Kafka in one thousand parables. It is said he composed them on days following his return to Prague from Berlin, where he traveled to visit his fiancée Felice Bauer. On such days Max Brod would often find Kafka brooding over a small black notebook and the remains of his modest breakfast. Kafka revealed the contents of the notebook only after unrelenting rib-jabbing and taunting by his friend, a service for which the literary world will forever be in Brod's debt.

The original notebook being lost, the sutras were reproduced from notes and memory by Brod in abbreviated form in five hundred chapters. This work was again lost, but not before being prepared for publication in an abridged form of one hundred and fifty chapters by that notoriously renegade Hasid, Bohdan ben-Zalman, a kettle-maker and publisher of erotica, curiosa, and illicit literature. These one hundred and fifty chapters were then put together under seven heads or parts named severally:

1. *Sadharana* (on general topics)
2. *Samprayogika* (on rejected advances, etc.)
3. *Kanya Samprayuktaka* (on advances not quite made in the first place)
4. *Bharyadhikarika* (on rejection by one's wife)
5. *Paradika* (on rejection by the wives of others)
6. *Vaisika* (on fear of approaching courtesans, and the memory of maternal injunctions regarding disease)

7. *Aupamishadika* (on the application of useless ointments)

The few copies of ben-Zalman's proofs having been variously suppressed, lost, destroyed, found, thoughtlessly repaired, amended, corrupted, ignored, and otherwise removed from the historical record, we find only these few fragments of the *Kafka Sutra* survive. They are here rendered into English for the first time, that we may partake of their wisdom and vision.

The Great Wall and the Tower of Babel

From the Bharyadhikarika.

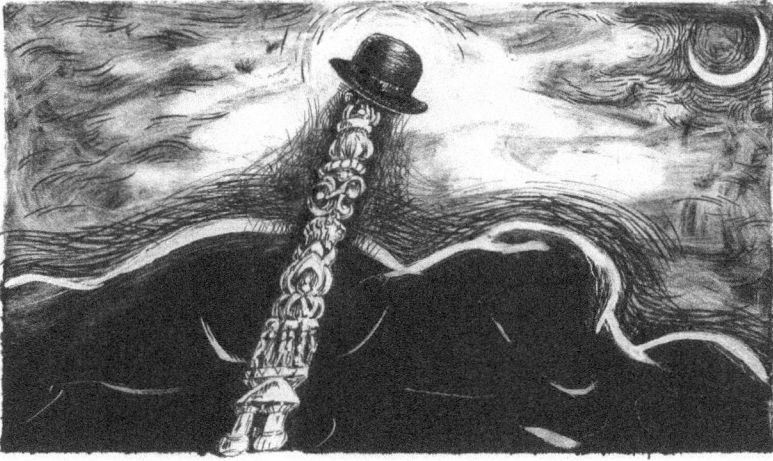

He is to attain, through weeks of restraint, desire such that a tumescence is achieved scarcely inferior to the unruined glory of the Tower of Babel and, as regards divine approval, not entirely at variance with that edifice. He lies supine, such that the monument of his desire towers above him.

She lies next to him, on her side, her back toward him, her curves and lavish limbs and silken surfaces forming in their long extension a Great Wall. She begins, softly, to snore.

He sees now that the tower failed because it was bound to fail.

An Imperial Message

From the Paradika.

She is an empress and sends him a message from the divan where, after the luxury of her bath, she stretches the magnificence of her flesh to be powdered by a favorite handmaiden. Her message, a summons of desire, is for him and him alone, her pathetic subject, a tiny shadow hidden at the farthest distance from her imperial sun. She orders her eunuch herald to kneel down beside the heat and delicate scent of her breast and, drawing him near, strokes his shaved head with a hand whose soft tautness itself promises fulfillments undreamed of by even the most jaded rakes among the courtly aristocrats. She whispers in the eunuch's jeweled ear words that cause him, a veteran of many years service and witness to countless debauches of the court, to blush. At her command the messenger whispers the message back to her, that she may confirm its accuracy. The words bear such promise of pleasure that he trembles in memory of his lost manhood. And there, in front of the attendant harem of handmaidens and silken ladies in waiting, she dispatches her herald with a commanding gesture of her bejeweled and opulent arm.

The messenger starts off at once, a powerfully built and tireless servant. Eyes and jaw set in determination, he elbows his way through the crowd of nubile bodies. Where he encounters resistance, he points to his breast, which bears the glittering sign of the imperial sun, and the crowd parts for him. But the crush of bodies is immense; the imperial dwelling infinite. If there were an open field, how he would fly along, and soon the intended would hear the pounding of his fist on the door. But instead, look how futile are all his efforts, how vainly he wastes his burly strength. He is still forcing his way through the private rooms of the innermost palace. Never will he win his way through. And if he did manage that, nothing would have been achieved. He would have to fight his way down the broad imperial steps, and, even if he managed to do that, still nothing would have been achieved, for the palace, which lies within the infinite city, has no end.

Out in the provinces the intended lies supine and contemplates with sorrow the Tower of Babel.

Leopards in the Temple

From the Samprayogika.

In leopardskin dresses they are to parade into the bar where he, smiling meekly, buys candy-colored drinks to slake their burning and majestic appetites. They sate themselves and drink to the very dregs, then, sleek-sided and tossing back their manes of gilded hair, abandon him.

This is repeated over and over again; it will be repeated forever. Blindly besotted, he is to understand it only as kind of foreplay.

Couriers

From the Kanya Samprayuktaka.

He is offered the choice of becoming a husband or the lover of another man's wife. Men being as they are, he wants to be a lover, as do all the others. Therefore there are only lovers hurrying around the world, near rabid with ardor and bearing their secret letters of desire. There being no husbands, though, there are no wives, so there is no one to receive their amorous messages. Secretly they would all like to put an end to this miserable way of life, but fear commitment.

The Coat of Arms

Erroneously appended to the Aupamishadika, *placed in the* Samprayogika *in the amended text, with an illustration since destroyed due to obscenity.*

Yearning to erect and revel in the glorious tumescence he terms the Tower of Babel, and to see that erection come to its fountain-jet of spasmed consummation, he sets out to lay the scene for seduction. All proceeds in good order; indeed, the order is perhaps too perfect, too much thought taken for silky acid jazz, wine choice, the softness of the lighting scheme, for whose books of experimental-but-sexy poems to leave on the coffee table—as if there were centuries to devote to such planning before getting on the job proper.

In fact, his general opinion is that one simply cannot plan one's lady-trap too slowly or with too much care; pushing the point the least bit further would have sufficed to make him hesitate to lay the foundations at all.

He philosophizes thusly: the essential thing in the whole business is the idea of laying the foundations that will allow the rearing a tower to breach the gates of connubial heaven. In comparison with that idea, everything else is secondary. This idea of a tower, once seized in its magnitude, can never vanish again; so long as there are men on the earth there will also be the irresistible desire to complete the tower. That being so, one need have no anxiety about the future; on the contrary, human knowledge is increasing, the art of seduction has made progress and will make further progress. A choice of body spray, a selection from one's supply of still-decent boxer shorts—these may take us a quarter hour but may perhaps be done in half the time in another hundred years, and better done, too, more effectively, enduringly.

So why, he thinks, exert oneself to the extreme limit of one's present powers? There would be some sense in doing that only if it were likely that the tower could be completed in one evening, on the first date. Impossible!

In thoughts of this fashion days and weeks pass, the scene of seduction unfinished.

It is for that reason that his coat of arms depicts a clenched fist closed round the Tower of Babel.

Before the Door

From the Vaisika.

Before the seedy entry to the brothel he finds a fat, greasy man on a discarded barstool. Having come from the countryside in great and urgent need, he asks the fat guard for entrance. But the guard says that it is not possible to admit him at just this moment. The man reflects briefly, then asks if he will be allowed to enter later on. "It *is* possible," says the gatekeeper, "just not at the moment." Since the door to the brothel stands open, as always, and the guard has turned toward the wall a little to shield the cigarette he's lighting from the wind, the man tries to catch a peek inside.

Seeing him, the guard laughs. "If you are so strongly tempted, try getting in despite my prohibition. But take note: I am powerful. And I am but the lowliest of the guards: from hall to hall wait guards at every door, each more terrifying than the last. By the time I get to the third door I can hardly stand to look at them myself." The countryman has not expected this—the brothel should be open to anyone prepared to pay. But when the man looks more closely at the guard and his coat trimmed with fake fur, his floppy hat, his gold-capped cane, his pointed eelskin boots and his long, thin, black Tartar's beard, it becomes clear that it would be better to wait for permission. The guard has given the countryman a little three-legged stool, much shorter than the barstool upon which his own bulk is massed, and gestures for the countryman to sit there at his side. There he sits for days and years, as the cold wind blows trash through the city's gutters. The man, who has equipped himself with many things for his journey to the city, slowly parts with everything he has, attempting time and again to bribe the gatekeeper. The latter accepts it all with a world-weary gaze, each time saying "I only take this so that you won't think there's anything you forgot to try."

The Ball Rider

From the Paradika.

*[In the most ancient extant text, perhaps in the hand of the elusive ben-Zalman, is the note "for ball, read ye bucket." Sages cannot explain this mystery.]

He is to sit all-but naked in his winter-cold room, on the edge of a narrow bed, one sock drooping low on a scrawny ankle, the other absent, bare branches outside the window, the sky itself an iron shield against any who look to it for comfort. Pitiful is his condition: he must have congress, and so must ride out beneath that uncaring sky seeking aid from his silken-limbed beloved, the dance of her tawny skin beneath his supplicating touch.

She is to have grown deaf to all ordinary appeals, such that he must demonstrate to her that he has not a single thought but his need, that her caress means to him the very sun in the firmament, a breaking of the iron chastity of the indifferent sky.

He must plan to approach like a starving beggar who, the death-rattle already risen in his throat, insists on expiring on her very doorstep. Like a beggar to whom the infinitely desired Sultana's cook decides to give the dregs of the coffee pot. The beloved, like this cook, must form her lips to a slight and contemptuous moue, but—and this is his hope, his aching dream—acknowledge nevertheless the dictum "Thou shall not kill," and fling with pity a little sugar his way. Maybe, just maybe, he is to tremblingly speculate, a hand-job.

His mode of arrival must decide the matter, so he rides off mounted on the swollen orbs within his scrotum. Buoyed upwards as if by a force greater than helium, he lays hands on his growing tumescence—the simplest of bridles—and so will propel himself with difficulty down the stairs, the bald and freckled spot atop his head scraping the ceiling. Once below, his billowing sack ascends superbly, superbly—camels humbly squatting on the ground do not rise with more dignity, shaking themselves under the sticks of their drivers. Through the hard frozen streets he goes at a regular canter; often upraised as high as the second story of a house; never is he to sink as low as the entrances.

At last he floats at an extraordinary height above the ceiling skylight of the beloved, whom he sees below, her elegant back in all its nakedness arched as she bends over a table, reading what looks unnervingly like a love note in another's hand. "Beloved!" he is to shout, in a voiced burned hollow by desire and shrouded in the cloud his hot breath makes in the night air, "please, beloved—be kind!"

Beneath the skylight she puts her hand to an ear exquisite as a butterfly beneath her magnificently curling tresses. "Do I hear something? A dying rabbit?" she will ask. She is then to throw on her sheerest sarong, angled like an arched eyebrow above the unattainable heaven of her hips, tied carelessly yet with an opulent grace, then cast open the window, and, insensate to the nasal whining of ongoing beseechments, let the sheer tulle, the satin of her voice sidle to his yearning ears. "Nothing," she will say, "there's nothing here; I see nothing, I hear nothing; only the clock striking, and now to bed. The cold is terrible; and tomorrow I'm promised a visitor."

She sees nothing and hears nothing; but all the same she loosens her sarong and waves it lightly, wafting him away. His steed has all the virtues of the best balloons or airships, save this: a woman's garment, wielded ever so slightly but with a minute ingenuity, sends it skittering through the air.

And so, his imploring overtures fading with the pale light of dawn, he ascends to the regions of ice-capped mountains—glimpsing below him the ruins of the Tower of Babel—and is lost.

Parables

Attributed to the Kanya Samprayuktaka.

He complains that the words of the sutras are merely parables and of no use in real life: "When the sage has written 'there she is, go get her, they're never happier than when they've got one up in 'em, etc.' the wise man does not mean that you should approach some actual hottie, but speaks of a philosophical Other, some transcendent object of ontological desire, something that the sage cannot designate any more precisely than we can. I mean, he can't actually help us at all. All these parables really set out to say is that the ineffable is ineffable, and we knew that already. But the aches of earthly desire: that's something else entirely."

She lies next to him, on her side, her back toward him, with her curves and lavish limbs and silken surfaces, and starts to snore.

17

II

RESPONSES

Sheena is a Punk Rocker

She, Sheena of the Jungle, the pulp-paged comics' great white queen,
she, Sheena, born in slumped-out England, born

for young Will Eisner's tabloid-writing scheme,
born of Jerry Eigner's drawing, Eisner's jiggle-in-the-jungle dream.

Reborn stateside nine months later (the money was better),
reborn a soft-core smash-hit shiksa, *Jumbo Comics'* break-out dame.

Born first in the blur of Eisner's novel-reading dreaming—
she, Sheena, born first in Rider Haggard's one-hand-novel *She.*

Sheena born in the blur of the movie-goer's dreaming
when Jeffrey Hyman (he'd drop Jeff, and go by Joey,

he'd drop Hyman, and then go by Ramone) caught her
in a seedy New York retro matinée:

kitsch TV for downtown's nascent highbrow-lowbrow scene.
She, Sheena of the big screen, born Nellie McCalla,

born the butcher's daughter (fifth of eight), she couldn't stay
in dull Pawnee, hopped it from her butcher father,

hopped the train from dull Pawnee.
Reborn in chic L.A., she, Sheena, she'd drop "Nellie,"

pose for Vargas, pose it well and beach-front, pose it well, and not
    for free.
"I couldn't act," says Sheena, "but I could swing from trees."

21

A pinned-up blonde, improbable as jungle queen,
improbable as her build, her frame, her curving fame, as in:

her 39-19-37, she, Sheena,
a big-screen screen-test six-foot queen.

She, Sheena, born again when Jeffrey (call him Joey) made
his infinitely probable 2 minutes forty, his infinitely perfect

four-chord *chart-this* scheme. Teens drive it up to 81,
in England make that 23. The hopped-up numbers scream

they know it: Sheena is a punk rocker, Sheena is
a punk rocker, Sheena is a punk rocker now.

Glam Rock: The Poem

From Mick Rock's famous photo of Bowie, Iggy, Lou, and manager.

1.

The man who was to fall to earth in four years' time
still floated in his cloud of silvered fame. His name

was David Robert Hayward Stenton Jones.
He'd been a Kon-Rad, King Bee, Manish Boy,

a Lower Third. He'd be a thin white duke.
He'd be a Christ, an alien, he'd be a dance club king.

Remembering the self-invented master whose factory
invented selves, he'd play in film the man who

played the soup-can trick on art, he'd play that man (not well).
He'd play the husband of a wife—she, born Somali,

she, born near Greece. He, born in Bromley, had one
real wife, she, born in Bromley, her girl's-mouth his,

the marriage bed that sweet narcissus mirror
where he'd play out all his parts.

These fragments has he shored against his gender, so.
His name was David Robert

Hayward Stenton Jones. Not David Jones, too close to Davey
of the pre-fab four. He'd change it first to Tom Jones, then again

and then again. But this year he was Ziggy,
this year he played guitar.

That's him on the left. The man who'd fall to earth,
camp in his arm-crook, his long neck's arch. Queer

in his gilded studied falsely vapid stare.
Nervous: glam and poise.

The others? That year he'd save them both.

2.
So New York and yet he's called "L.A."
when he fronts the Eldorados at a dance. He'd been a Jade,

be mother nature's son, but been a Jade who sang
a doo-wop plaintive "Leave Her for Me."

And she was Lisa and she'd say. And she was Stephanie
who'd also say. And she was Jane and Candy too,

or she would be. But he was Delmore Schwartz's
best student, gone to smack and speed and hell,

and he'd come back. He'd play the White House
for two presidents, one ours, and one

the velvet revolutionary who'd call him the Velvet Underground's
own JFK, own wild-side walking Mao or Che.

A three-chord Che? No martyr—though he'd bottom out.
He'd always be the cracked-id island suburb kid who double-coded

his libido's twists in "CHD," his high school band: the
    backward-reading acronym
for Dry Hump Club: three boys, a girl, and one guitar.

One guitar lesson's all he'd need, a Carl Perkins 1-4-5 he'd play.
He'd play too much with fire, the kind

his "mashed-faced Negro friend, called Jaw"
sold him, with hepatitis, early on.

He'd play five years with his best band.
He'd leave and play out on his own (not well).

He's on the right, behind his shades, behind the junkie act
in which the junkie hides.

Nervous: cold-edged poise.
Bowie'd helped him make *Transformer*.

Reed's cracked id made his music well again.

3.
He'd write "China Girl," and he'd sing "Shades"
the second time the thin man fell to earth

to scoop him up. His name was Pop. Had been Osterberg, had
been Prime Mover, had briefly been Iguana,

would then be Pop. Twice called by Stooge, first
psychedelic, later (times where changing) not.

The Idiot who'd Lust for Life. Like the Velvets
but not all cerebellum: all burnout, bastard, broke-ass bum.

A pack of Luckies in his teeth. His arms around them both,
a drunken sailor Jesus carried, his forward thrust

and their support. His eyes say "yes" his eyes say "now"
his eyes say "no one drives this drunken car." And they're in love.

The attraction? The man called Stardust, star-struck, said
"not Iggy in but Iggy and," and the Stooges drop to second bill,

while Iggy's resurrected (still on smack).
The wonder of attraction? Not his chops—

he tried for ten months, played Chicago blues (not well).
And not his lyrics, his "Mona" or his "TV Eye". *Raw Power*. For
    this,

Ziggy'd play his management, get Ig a gig, a big release.
Lou Reed gave his producer: chops, technique, tribute, and joy.

The wonder of attraction?
Not nervous, not with poise, not him.

No one to drive the car.

4.
Perspective's trick's a little imp behind their shoulders:
Tony Defries. He's thinking

"Hammersmith Odeon," thinking "aren't they
fun!" He's thinking, too "but will it sell?"

and then he's smiling, thinking, "yes."

La Bandera

It's in America (that is, the U.S.A.), that I have landed,
clutching my cars and TIAA-CREF,
my yellow-shingled house perched on its acre lot.

Which means? Which means? Which means the things I've seen
are wonderful, and sinister,
and many, many are the spangled flags.

I have seen them by the lakes and oceans, stiff,
with growing confidence, high in air; I have seen them
on the beaches, the landing grounds, I have seen them

in the fields and streets. They will never surrender.
I have seen them on ball-caps, plastic cups, on napkins
(on days not yet the fourth, in months not yet July),

seen them brazen on the mud-flaps of eighteen-wheelers,
on the foil packets of moist towelettes and, once, once, a pair of
    them,
tattooed on a stripper's spreading, well-toned inner thighs.

(Once? No, twice. Oh furtiveness, oh sneaking back).
I have seen Canadian flags, but they were in Canada,
and on flagpoles, too. They do things differently up there.

I've seen, too, *la bandera*, the flag of Mexico.
With its eagle, born before Columbus, born as the sun.
Born for Tenochtitlan.

The eagle's claw-clutched serpent born for Aztecs,
who called it wisdom,
born with a hiss called "whispered truth."

Later, born again for brazen Spaniards, and born royal:
águila real, the eagle clutched the writhing pagan serpent, and
perched brazen in the center, in the white field of the
    revolution's tricolor.

Which means? Which means? A sneaking in
of church and crown, surviving, there (they never surrender)
surviving, brazen—a claw hangs on.

But that's not where I saw them, not at first.
I saw them on my father's forearm, saw them, tattooed, there.
Saw them as both wonderful, and sinister. Saw them,

and didn't know. And didn't know how, back from the Marines
—back from the beaches, the landing grounds,
the fields and streets, the *never surrender*—he swore off

the land of yellow-shingled houses, and all their acre lots,
took flight for Mexico, and beatniked there.
His perch, where he had landed, and for good,

or so he thought. And then? And then?
A furtiveness? A sneaking back.
A spreading land of many spangled flags.

What Heart Heard Of, Ghost Guessed

You don't quite notice till you do. Like lately,
how I just don't hear my daughter say the things

she used to say. She's five. And not too long ago,
when her tiny top-knot face would go bright red,

the frustrations of the twitchy little will all boiled up,
the cherry tomato of her head would howl

for me to stop. "Never!" she'd shriek, and "I command you!"
I'm sure she picked it up from some cartoon,

along with "to the car!" and "to the beach!"—
some superhero talk, some melodrama. And there I'd be,

charmed, and choking back a laugh. Of course she was wild
with anger (what decent parents call *"upset"*). Of course I'd want
    to help.

I mean, one cares. But I'd always also think how cute, how not-
    quite-right,
how much she meant that campy "I command you!"

and wanted it to work, how deep it rooted
in a buried, red-toothed rage, a kraken torn from all its sunken
    sleep.

And just because I'd combed her snaggled hair,
or taken her to swim or ride her bike: violations

of unmediated desire. She's changed.
I feel the thing all fathers feel: we wouldn't want to hold them
    back.

They'll say new things. And mine? She'll better know what works
when pairing words with what we feel. She'll know too well,

and work me round, get what she wants. I know.
That's as it should be, right? Okay. But

she doesn't say the things she used to say. She's changed—
and something red-faced and unreasonable, balking, some
    kraken shriek

inside me seeks its words, and wants to shout (to whom?)
"Stop!" and "I command you!" and "Stop!" and "Never! Stop!"

We Must Not Say So

Poem for a book about John Berryman.

Sadness was he ever. Teacher, taught
my teacher, taught me too (this being not
in body but in book). "What is the boy now
who has lost his ball?" he'd ask. The question's flawed.
"What, what" he'd ask "is he to do?" A haughty Henry'd
huff his loss, a stone his daily broken bread.
And yours and mine? Is what he wrought?
Sadness we are ever, teacher taught.

"No use," he'd say, to say "O, there
are other balls," the ball gone harbor-wise,
and out, the tidal-tugging way.
No use to whistle "I am not a little boy."
For him a hurting. Us, maybe a sigh.
No laws against our Henry but "Beware."

Robert Archambeau

English Majors

Poem for a darker season.

They disappoint me, bore me, do, the dutiful
daughters; bore me, too, those disappointing sons.
As I bore them. And that they do not know,
not care—it wears the worst of all. They do not
do for this old shoe (achoo). *Pace* Plath, I'd tell them, once,
again, again, again. Perhaps I'd better call the poem (if 'poem'
    we wish it called) then,
"Youth." Or "Middle Age."

Lecture Hall

Oh trustees and committees, I am not he!

If it were a single lecture hall, tall-tiered
    and gloomy-lighted, your career ...
If you were pacing in the well-pit smear of light,
    your notes, your plans ...
If all your students, from then and now,
    from years filed in chalk-dust corridors
had filtered in and filled the curving tiers
    of that great hall ... Not coming as they are,
aged, aging, youthful still but moving on,
    but as they were: eighteen, or all of twenty-one,
a backpack-toting crowd of shuffling notes ...
    Where would you put them, how assign the seats?
The back for half-seen shadowed faces, half-remembered
    from those class lists of years ago,
before their mortgages, or fellowships, before the tumor,
    or the sailboat bought to flee the life not lived.
The front for those who, just last semester, earned an "A"
    on Yeats, a well-meant "C" on Blake,
who called you late at night, or hardly showed at all.
    Clear name-and-features match-ups,
learned early in the course and not forgotten
    yet. Up front for those, their hat-brims bent,
their sneaker-shuffle, sweats and arguments
    about who'd have the lead part in the play. Them, near the
    front.
But not the first row, not for them, not that, reserved
    for those who mattered in the ways they shouldn't,
ways you couldn't let them know,

33

or did, the ones you had back to your house,
the ones you could have loved,
    or did, the ones who wanted
just to smoke a joint and talk.
    The laddish talk of men who'd be your friends.
For her, red-haired, her scarf wrapped round that pale long throat
    in some Parisian knot you'd never quite unravel, for him,
the anger-eyed and dark-haired boy you knew
    from years before, his black clothes yours,
for them, the front-row seats,
    a touch too close to stage.

Sestina: What Chester Kallman Did to Poor Old Auden

Your note asked me to weed your savage garden,
To revise and edit, like the old man Auden,
Whose best, and lying, lines were cut—ejected
And chucked from "Spain." Well, it's your villa,
And weeding's not high rent. The view's seducing—
But chastely so. Not like your secretary

Who did the poster-pose from *Secretary*
When I came in, post-weeding of the garden.
Her backside did to me, in that seducing,
What Chester Kallman's did to poor old Auden:
I gasped like Saint Teresa of Avilla
(Bernini's, not de Beauvoir's, who ejected

All men, all sex, all but herself—ejected
All but privacy, a secretary
To God, who rarely called). So, at your villa
My hand dropped down those weeds torn from your garden—
I reached, instead, for some bright words of Auden,
In hope, redundant hope, that some seducing

Line would match that pose, itself seducing.
But each was neck-scruff caught, rudely ejected—
My mind a discotheque, those lines of Auden
Bounced out by rough Lust. Your secretary
Glanced back, rose, and slithered to the garden,
That apple orchard there around your villa.

I should have mentioned that: your fine old villa
Being allegorical. Seducing
Is what happens in Edenic Gardens.
We're here to kiss, and then (fate!) be ejected;
Why else would she be game, this secretary?
"Eve and Adam, till the Fall," said Auden,

"Were illogical." *That* line of Auden
Got through well enough. Logic, at your villa,
Suspends itself. Sleek secretaries,
Apple-derrièred, who go seducing
Portly, graying poets would be ejected
From reason's trim and (say it) arid garden:

Auden knew it. About all that seducing:
It's your villa—will I be ejected?
Your secretary fucked me in your garden.

"It is an ancient Mariner, And he stoppeth one of three ..."

i.m. Joyce Kilmer

The guys in the reflective orange
    vests who are setting up the
trellis on the esplanade of the
    Botanic Garden are not setting up
the trellis; they are lounging like a
    group of figures sculpted by
Bernini and laughing at the
    ducks playing in the mist from the
fountain. And the guy taking
    notes in the margins of a book of
poems is not taking notes but
    smiling at the guys laughing at
the ducks and you are not
    reading this poem but smiling at the
guy—no, you're reading this poem. Sorry.
    Go outside.

Working the Piano

For John Matthias, after writing on his work for many years

"One does not work the piano,
or the violin. One does not create a body

of play." I read this
in another poet's poem, and think of you. Not

when I first knew you, in those classes that you thought of
as your work, your job, not later

when you supervised (such work!) my work,
my PhD—I thought of you at nine

or twelve years old, Republican Ohio, say, in 1950
or in 1953. In

costume, all the sticks and staves,
the plumed hat, fencing foil, your cape, your cousin

dressed the same, the world you opened
every summer, lovely and legitimate,

that world of play.
And if it is your work

my books are all about,
then you have worked the piano thirty years and more,

have worked the violin,
have worked with sticks and staves and fencing foil

to build a world both lovely and legitimate:
a jeweled box, a field of wrens

where, while you don't know it,
I and others wander and return.

Robert Archambeau

The Poem That Does Not Exist

The poem that does not exist walks into a bar.
"Knock knock," it says, to get to the other side.
The poem that does not exist is all you can eat
driving through the drive thru.

The poem that does not exist "falls upon the thorns of life,"
it reads.
The poem that does not exist as distichs
shops for its organic form at the organic farm.

The poem that does not exist exits,
but it's the wrong exit. Fucking GPS.
Anxious that it has missed its audience,
the poem that does not exist loops back to line one to start again,

but, finding a volta in a cup holder just when it needs one,
hurls the coin at the toll basket & turns away.

Letter To Albert Goldbarth

Remixing and writing-through Budget Travel
through Space and Time

I ate your book, Albert,
or should I say:
I ate your book the way the snake
in your poem ate its mouse:
first, the slow survey of rich terrain,
then somehow
without an indication of speed
or even movement (it was easy:
I was stretched out on the couch)
I gulped the living thing
down whole. But that's not right.
Your book's no mouse, but
something supple and absorptive,
something setting out to take it all,
like the topless dancer who took your pal
for all his tens and twenties, all his fives and ones,
who, playful, took his quarters and his dimes.
I think I came across the book in Mexico,
when I lived in a village so small I always thought
a rain of more than an hour would wash it
into the jungle totally, with its one telephone,
its butcher knife, its five flutes
and handful of silt. I don't know why I was there,
or if it even happened,
or if it only happened in the book I'd swallowed whole.
I don't know why my hunger took me there,
unless it had to do with how the words I'd been born into

weren't enough,
and I'd come because I wanted more inside me,
more digestion stones, like what an owl has, and more
for them to go to pulverizing work on.
I ate your book, Albert.
But that's not right:
I write inside the belly of a snake.

Cooking Without Milton

For John Milton, his neologisms.

… there'd be none of it. Nor would the army's airborne leap.
Nor could the sensuous love-lorn, half-starved for what they
    lacked,
hot-headed or cherubic, lapse into complacency—
it's true. Six hundred words, or maybe more,
first unfurled their syllables to readers (jubilant,
ungenerous, or dismissive) of Milton's adamantine verse.
And no such reader's jubilance, nor ungenerosity, nor her
    dismissiveness
could be, had he not wrote. Nor could we fall
to debauchery unaccountable, or depravity unprincipled,
however much we (oh arch-fiends that we are, or can be, since
    he wrote)
might try. At least there'd be no chastening.
So let all fallen and unfallen angels sing besottedly,
and long, that Milton epistled, prelatised, and intervolved
opiniastrously. We'd have no pandemonium without him.

Robert Archambeau

Brightness Falls

Remembering another war: for Dubravka in Belgrade, April 1999.

"Brightness falls from the air"
wrote Thomas Nashe, in his poem
on the plague. For "air" read "hair,"

that's what he meant: the glossless
stuff of age, of death.
Someone had blundered:

the mis-set type, the blotted word,
the error stirred a dead-dull line
to breath and strange truth-ringing life.

And when our bombers flew south
and I tapped out hurried, guilty words
to warn you that they came,

your message scrolled up on my screen
"Thank you for warring."
For "warring" read "warning,"

I know, I know. But that night
of error, of fear-stirred death,
a brightness fell from all your air.

Hieratic Perspective

I went into the cathedral that was for me alone,
where the guide who was also for me alone,

and of me alone, spoke to me alone
of the niche-bound altarpiece

that mapped my spirit out for me.
He said:

"God's holy fire, sure, is in these
panels, damaged, gold, and glorious,

perched in the cathedral only you
have ever stepped in

(you and I are here—right!—
but you and I are one, if even that).

So look what's there, on the altarpiece,
its images, Italo-Byzantine,

in that gold-on-gold terrarium, the angel ant-farm
of that flattened space. A clustering of haloed heads,

consecrate, and hallowed, and decayed.
Front and center, at six foot eight,

almost the full height of the panel, there:
blue-robed and bulky: your libido,

the fine-drawn bright bits
chipped away—a blue tempura

never lasts. We cannot
tell the gender, anymore, if it were ever manifest

(sources are vague, and disagree, and written
by monks—what would they know?). Bloated,

faceless, it keeps the object of desire there,
dandled on its knee— she's smudged-up

by the candle smoke, a little limb is left, you see, a little
pink-fleshed arm, a haunch, and something of a mouth,

quite cruel.
The tiny putti dancing at her feet are appetites,

so many I've often asked myself
'was there an explosion at the cherub factory?'

And kneeling, off to either side: the patrons. If they stood
they wouldn't reach that central figure's knees.

They paid for this. You know them, too: the people
that you owe. And then behind:

their clustered heads a mass of dazzled haloed light,
the patron saints of work, and reputation,

of jokes and reefer, drink, and hanging out, the patron saint
of art. What are they? Two foot three? A choir

to sing and cry for you. To look upward
at that high-placed panel that was never painted,

or (here sources disagree)
we've lost."

*

I went into the cathedral that was for me alone,
where the guide who was also for me alone,

and of me alone,
spoke to me alone,

and to himself, who was also me alone,
and I looked away, to where curled smoke

sleep-walked and grew tall and taller
above the altar,

wove ropes around itself, and disappeared.

Nag Hammadi: A Parable

It's night: the watchman discovers a thief in the fields.
They fight, the thief is slain, but his kinsman kills the watchman
    in revenge.
The watchman's sons find the dead thief's kinsman selling
    molasses in the market.
They hack him to pieces with their mattocks. They eat his heart.
    It's day.
It's true—it's Egypt, 1945. No one would speak against them—
some silent from fear, some choked with hatred of the dead
    man and his kin.
Months pass. The watchman's sons stalk slowly through dry hills.
They find a cave, and a red jar, very old.
Is it heavy with gold? Does it cage a demon?
The elder brother conjures courage, hoists his mattock, smashes
    down.
Below the whirling dust are 13 books—cracked and ancient,
    without sense
(no one taught these brothers how to read). Books hiss as
    kindling in their mother's oven.
By chance, a Coptic priest comes. He saves what few remain.
They are relics of the bygone Gnostics—the *Apocryphon of James*,
the *Tripartite Tractate*, the *Treatise on the Resurrection*.
They have nothing in common but this: each declares the evil of
    this world.

III

TWO PROCEDURES

Manifest Destinies, Black Rains

Source texts:
Anne C. Lynch, "A Sketch of Washington City,"
Harper's New Monthly Magazine December 1852;
Masuji Ibuse, *Black Rain*, 1965.

With the broadest principles of freedom for the foundation of our government—with a magnificent country, whose shores are washed by the great oceans, whose lakes are seas, whose rivers are the most majestic that water the earth, whose commerce whitens every sea, whose railroads and canals, like great arteries, intersect its whole surface, and carry life and activity to its remotest corner; whose "magnetic nerves," with the rapidity of thought, bear intelligence to its distant extremities; with a people springing from the fusion of many races, and whose energies are as inexhaustible as the resources of the country they inhabit, it would seem that here the human mind is destined to develop its highest powers, and that, while on one side its influence will roll back upon the tottering monarchies of Europe, on the other its advancing tide of freedom and civilization will stretch across the Pacific, to the shores of Asia, and pour upon them its fertilizing flood.

—*Washington*

We reached the streetcar stop at Kamiya-cho. The streetcar tracks crossed each other here, and broken overhead wires and cables hung down in tangled profusion over the road. I had a terrifying feeling that one or the other of them must be live, since these were the same wires that one usually saw emitting fierce, bluish white sparks. The occasional refugees who passed to and fro had the sense to crouch down as they passed beneath them.

Mr. Omuro was a man of property, owning mills in three different places, as well as dabbling in calligraphy, painting, and art-collecting. I had visited the house myself several times during the past year for the benefit of his advice.... Now, however, it was completely razed to the ground. Where the main building and clay-walled storehouse had once stood was an arid waste scattered with broken tiles.

    —*Hiroshima*

[1-1]

A magnificent country, whose commerce whitens every sea,
whose most majestic railroads and canals, like great arteries,
    hang down, broken, in tangled profusion—
I had a terrifying feeling that one or another of them must
be live, fierce.

[1-2]

A man of property dabbling in painting and art collecting,
a man of property whose commerce whitens every sea,
a man of property with the broadest principles of freedom,
a man of property whose railroads carry occasional refugees.

[1-3]

A magnificent country's principles of freedom,
completely razed to the ground.
Where they had once stood an arid waste
Scattered with broken tiles.

[2-1]

Here, it seemed, the human mind was destined to develop its
    highest powers.
Here, it seemed, in the inexhaustible country they inhabit.
Magnetic nerves, with the rapidity of thought, bore intelligence
    to distant extremities. I had a terrifying feeling
the mind was destined to spark and tangle: fierce and white.

[2-2]

Here, with a people springing from the fusion of many races,
      the human mind is destined to develop its highest powers
of thought. Calligraphy, painting, art-collecting.
An intelligence inexhaustible
as a man of property owning mills in three different places.

Robert Archambeau

[2-3]

A people springing from many races is destined.
A people springing from inexhaustible ground is destined.
From fission, a distant people, razed.
From fission an arid waste is destined, and broken tiles.

[3-1]

Stretched across the Pacific, tottering,
we pour upon them, roll back on the tide.
A terrifying feeling, advancing.
Tangled, broken, we reach the fierce shores of Asia.

Robert Archambeau

[3-2]

To the Pacific, to the shores of Asia,
to pour upon them the sense of civilization,
the sense of freedom advancing. On one side of the
flood the tottering refugees had the sense to crouch.

[3-3]

Now, where the tottering had stood,
clay-walled Asia was completely razed to the ground.
The storehouse scattered, broken
in the advancing tide, the fertilizing flood.

If Wronging You Is Love

Conceptualist inversion of Felix Bernstein's "If Loving You Is Wrong," dedicated to Mr. Bernstein (14,100 results), by Mr. Archambeau (18,300 results).

If Andy Warhol (16,300,000 results) is a poet, I don't want to be a poet

If Socrates (7,700,000 results) is a poet, I don't want to be a poet

If Homer (4,160,000 results) is a poet, I don't want to be a poet

If Emily Dickinson (980,000 results) is a poet, I don't want to be a poet

If Robert Frost (812,000 results) is a poet, I don't want to be a poet

If Langston Hughes (754,000 results) is a poet, I don't want to be a poet

If Walt Whitman (732,000 results) is a poet, I don't want to be a poet

If Maya Angelou (722,000 results) is a poet, I don't want to be a poet

If Sylvia Plath (547,000 results) is a poet, I don't want to be a poet

If William Wordsworth (526,000 results) is a poet, I don't want to be a poet

If Charles Bukowski (523,000 results) is a poet, I don't want to be a poet

If Allen Ginsberg (521,000 results) is a poet, I don't want to be a poet

If Jack Kerouac (497,000 results) is a poet, I don't want to be a poet

If Dante Alighieri (417,000) is a poet, I don't want to be a poet

If Billy Collins (410,000 results) is a poet, I don't want to be a poet

If John Cage (375,000 results) is a poet, I don't want to be a poet

If Frank O'Hara (361,000 results) is a poet, I don't want to be a poet

If Robert Lowell (363,000 results) is a poet, I don't want to be a poet

If Catullus (355,000 results) is a poet, I don't want to be a poet

If Anne Sexton (339,000 results) is a poet, I don't want to be a poet

If Adrienne Rich (323,000 results) is a poet, I don't want to be a poet

If Mary Oliver (310,000 results) is a poet, I don't want to be a poet

If John Ashbery (243,000 results) is a poet, I don't want to be a poet

If Rae Armantrout (224,000 results) is a poet, I don't want to be a poet

If Amiri Baraka (224,000 results) is a poet, I don't want to be a poet

If Gary Snyder (216,000 results) is a poet, I don't want to be a poet

If Robert Hass (169,000 results) is a poet, I don't want to be a poet

If Audre Lorde (166,000 results) is a poet, I don't want to be a poet

If Lawrence Ferlinghetti (158,000 results) is a poet, I don't want to be a poet

If W.S. Merwin (155,000 results) is a poet, I don't want to be a poet

If Charles Simic (149,000 results) is a poet, I don't want to be a poet

If Rita Dove (148,000 results) is a poet, I don't want to be a poet

If Robert Creeley (147,000 results) is a poet, I don't want to be a poet

If Denise Levertov (143,000 results) is a poet, I don't want to be a poet

If Robert Pinsky (141,000 results) is a poet, I don't want to be a poet

If Charles Bernstein (129,000 results) is a poet, I don't want to be a poet

If Robert Duncan (122,000 results) is a poet, I don't want to be a poet

If Charles Olson (116,000 results) is a poet, I don't want to be a poet

If David Lehman (112,000 results) is a poet, I don't want to be a poet

If Gregory Corso (101,000 results) is a poet, I don't want to be a poet

If Charles Wright (99,500 results) is a poet, I don't want to be a poet

If Mark Doty (98,400 results) is a poet, I don't want to be a poet

If Kay Ryan (87,100 results) is a poet, I don't want to be a poet

If Jerome Rothenberg (84,000 results) is a poet, I don't want to be a poet

If Bill Corbett (82,600 results) is a poet, I don't want to be a poet

If Kenneth Koch (79,500 results) is a poet, I don't want to be a poet

If Ron Silliman (78,700 results) is a poet, I don't want to be a poet

If Anne Waldman (77,300 results) is a poet, I don't want to be a poet

If Tom Clark (75,300 results) is a poet, I don't want to be a poet

If Natasha Trethewey (70,800 results) is a poet, I don't want to be a poet

If Jack Spicer (68,400 results) is a poet, I don't want to be a poet

If Jim Carroll (65,400 results) is a poet, I don't want to be a poet

Robert Archambeau

If Michael Palmer (65,000 results) is a poet, I don't want to be a poet
If Michael McClure (62,300 results) is a poet, I don't want to be a poet
If James Laughlin (58,100 results) is a poet, I don't want to be a poet
If Jorie Graham (58,600 results) is a poet, I don't want to be a poet
If Susan Howe (58,000 results) is a poet, I don't want to be a poet
If Philip Whalen (57,400 results) is a poet, I don't want to be a poet
If Andrei Codrescu (56,200 results) is a poet, I don't want to be a poet
If Tao Lin (51,300 results) is a poet, I don't want to be a poet
If Eileen Myles (51,200 results) is a poet, I don't want to be a poet
If Ted Berrigan (50,300 results) is a poet, I don't want to be a poet
If Lyn Hejinian (48,800 results) is a poet, I don't want to be a poet
If Robert Kelly (46,500 results) is a poet, I don't want to be a poet
If Clayton Eshleman (46,200 results) is a poet, I don't want to be a poet
If Ron Padgett (45,700 results) is a poet, I don't want to be a poet
If Leslie Scalapino (45,100 results) is a poet, I don't want to be a poet
If Ed Sanders (43,400 results) is a poet, I don't want to be a poet
If Kenneth Goldsmith (42,600 results) is a poet, I don't want to be a poet
If Diane di Prima (42,600 results) is a poet, I don't want to be a poet
If Alice Notley (42,300 results) is a poet, I don't want to be a poet
If C.D. Wright (40,300 results) is a poet, I don't want to be a poet
If James Schuyler (40,300 results) is a poet, I don't want to be a poet
If Dennis Cooper (40,100 results) is a poet, I don't want to be a poet
If Nathaniel Mackey (36,900 results) is a poet, I don't want to be a poet
If Steve McCaffery (35,500 results) is a poet, I don't want to be a poet
If Laura Moriarty (34,100 results) is a poet, I don't want to be a poet
If George Evans (32,500 results) is a poet, I don't want to be a poet
If John Giorno (32,500 results) is a poet, I don't want to be a poet
If Rosmarie Waldrop (31,900 results) is a poet, I don't want to be a poet
If Jimmy Santiago Baca (31,800 results) is a poet, I don't want to be a poet

If Ben Lerner (30,000 results) is a poet, I don't want to be a poet
If Fanny Howe (29,400 results) is a poet, I don't want to be a poet
If Peter Gizzi (28,900 results) is a poet, I don't want to be a poet
If Barbara Guest (28,800) results) is a poet, I don't want to be a poet
If David Shapiro (28,800 results) is a poet, I don't want to be a poet
If Bruce Andrews (28,300 results) is a poet, I don't want to be a poet
If Wanda Coleman (28,200 results) is a poet, I don't want to be a poet
If Jackson Mac Low (28,200 results) is a poet, I don't want to be a poet
If Harryette Mullen (28,000 results) is a poet, I don't want to be a poet
If Bernadette Mayer (27,900 results) is a poet, I don't want to be a poet
If Linh Dinh (27,700 results) is a poet, I don't want to be a poet
If Clark Coolidge (27,500 results) is a poet, I don't want to be a poet
If John Yau (27,300 results) is a poet, I don't want to be a poet
If Hilda Morley (27,200 results) is a poet, I don't want to be a poet
If Diane Wakoski (26,500 results) is a poet, I don't want to be a poet
If David Antin (26,200 results) is a poet, I don't want to be a poet
If Lisa Jarnot (25,800 results) is a poet, I don't want to be a poet
If Anselm Hollo (25,400 results) is a poet, I don't want to be a poet
If Bob Perelman (25,300 results) is a poet, I don't want to be a poet
If Norma Cole (24,700 results) is a poet, I don't want to be a poet
If Elizabeth Robinson (24,700 results) is a poet, I don't want to be a poet
If Paul Hoover (24,000 results) is a poet, I don't want to be a poet
If Claudia Rankine (23,800 results) is a poet, I don't want to be a poet
If Jayne Cortez (23,600 results) is a poet, I don't want to be a poet
If Paul Blackburn (23,500 results) is a poet, I don't want to be a poet
If Cole Swensen (23,400 results) is a poet, I don't want to be a poet
If John Godfrey (22,700 results) is a poet, I don't want to be a poet
If August Kleinzahler (22,100 results) is a poet, I don't want to be a poet
If Andrew Joron (22,000 results) is a poet, I don't want to be a poet

If Ed Dorn (21,800 results) is a poet, I don't want to be a poet
If Barrett Watten (21,900 results) is a poet, I don't want to be a poet
If Clarence Major (21,800 results) is a poet, I don't want to be a poet
If Elaine Equi (21,700 results) is a poet, I don't want to be a poet
If Vanessa Place (21,600 results) is a poet, I don't want to be a poet
If Lorenzo Thomas (20,800 results) is a poet, I don't want to be a poet
If Susan Wheeler (20,800 results) is a poet, I don't want to be a poet
If Russell Edson (20,700 results) is a poet, I don't want to be a poet
If Wang Ping (20,500 results) is a poet, I don't want to be a poet
If Art Lange (20,200 results) is a poet, I don't want to be a poet
If Will Alexander (20,000 results) is a poet, I don't want to be a poet
If Michael Davidson (19,900 results) is a poet, I don't want to be a poet
If Bill Berkson (19,800 results) is a poet, I don't want to be a poet
If Gillian Conoley (19,400 results) is a poet, I don't want to be a poet
If Amy Gerstler (19,100 results) is a poet, I don't want to be a poet
If Nada Gordon (19,000 results) is a poet, I don't want to be a poet
If CA Conrad (18,700 results) is a poet, I don't want to be a poet
If Catherine Wagner (18,500 results) is a poet, I don't want to be a poet
If Brian Kim Stefans (18,000 results) is a poet, I don't want to be a poet
If Keith Waldrop (18,000 results) is a poet, I don't want to be a poet
If K. Silem Mohammad (17,900 results) is a poet, I don't want to be a poet
If Jessica Hagedorn (17,400 results) is a poet, I don't want to be a poet
If Mark McMorris (17,000 results) is a poet, I don't want to be a poet
If Ann Lauterbach (16,900 results) is a poet, I don't want to be a poet
If Miguel Algarín (16,700 results) is a poet, I don't want to be a poet
If Robert Grenier (16,500 results) is a poet, I don't want to be a poet
If Ronald Johnson (16,400 results) is a poet, I don't want to be a poet
If Eleni Sikélianòs (15,800 results) is a poet, I don't want to be a poet
If Christian Bök (15,700 results) is a poet, I don't want to be a poet

If Craig Dworkin (15,400 results) is a poet, I don't want to be a poet

If John Wieners (15,100 results) is a poet, I don't want to be a poet

If Maxine Chernoff (15,000 results) is a poet, I don't want to be a poet

If Mei-mei Berssenbrugge (15,000 results) is a poet, I don't want to be a poet

If Edwin Torres (14,400 results) is a poet, I don't want to be a poet

If Tan Lin (14,400 results) is a poet, I don't want to be a poet

If Donald Revell (14,300 results) is a poet, I don't want to be a poet

If Hannah Weiner (13,700 results) is a poet, I don't want to be a poet

If Elizabeth Willis (13,500 results) is a poet, I don't want to be a poet

If Larry Eigner (13,100 results) is a poet, I don't want to be a poet

If Joshua Marie Wilkinson (13,000 results) is a poet, I don't want to be a poet

If Joan Retallack (12,900 results) is a poet, I don't want to be a poet

If Carla Harryman (12,400 results) is a poet, I don't want to be a poet

If Noah Eli Gordon (12,200 results) is a poet, I don't want to be a poet

If Kathleen Fraser (12,100 results) is a poet, I don't want to be a poet

If Paul Violi (11,300 results) is a poet, I don't want to be a poet

If Gary Sullivan (11,300 results) is a poet, I don't want to be a poet

If G.C. Waldrep (11,100 results) is a poet, I don't want to be a poet

If Julie Carr (11,000 results) is a poet, I don't want to be a poet

If Maureen Owen (10,900 results) is a poet, I don't want to be a poet

If Charles North (10,700 results) is a poet, I don't want to be a poet

If Kenward Elmslie (10,600 results) is a poet, I don't want to be a poet

If Myung Mi Kim (10,100 results) is a poet, I don't want to be a poet

If Sharon Mesmer (10,100 results) is a poet, I don't want to be a poet

If Gustaf Sobin (9,720 results) is a poet, I don't want to be a poet

If Bin Ramke (9,530 results) is a poet, I don't want to be a poet

If Victor Hernández Cruz (9,380 results) is a poet, I don't want to be a poet

If Joseph Ceravolo (9,150 results) is a poet, I don't want to be a poet

If Stephen Rodefer (9,130 results) is a poet, I don't want to be a poet

If Jennifer Moxley (8,940 results) is a poet, I don't want to be a poet
If Rusty Morrison (8,840 results) is a poet, I don't want to be a poet
If Laura Mullen (8,830 results) is a poet, I don't want to be a poet
If Laynie Browne (8,390 results) is a poet, I don't want to be a poet
If Noelle Kocot (8,290 results) is a poet, I don't want to be a poet
If Katie Degentesh (8,260 results) is a poet, I don't want to be a poet
If Stacy Doris (8,110 results) is a poet, I don't want to be a poet
If Stephen Ratcliffe (7,980 results) is a poet, I don't want to be a poet
If Tony Towle (7,880 results) is a poet, I don't want to be a poet
If Drew Gardner (7,740 results) is a poet, I don't want to be a poet
If Diane Ward (7,600 results) is a poet, I don't want to be a poet
If Graham Foust (6,800 results) is a poet, I don't want to be a poet
If Ray DiPalma (6,490 results) is a poet, I don't want to be a poet
If Joseph Lease (6,190 results) is a poet, I don't want to be a poet
If Aaron Shurin (6,180 results) is a poet, I don't want to be a poet
If Marjorie Welish (6,110 results) is a poet, I don't want to be a poet
If Ed Roberson (6,100 results) is a poet, I don't want to be a poet
If Tom Mandel (5,150 results) is a poet, I don't want to be a poet
If Claudia Keelan (4,280 results) is a poet, I don't want to be a poet
If Caroline Knox (4,120 results) is a poet, I don't want to be a poet
If Rob Fitterman (3,620 results) is a poet, I'll consider it
If C.S. Giscombe (2,860 results) is a poet, I want to be a poet

IV

VERSIONS

Translations, free and loose, impossible
without the collaboration of Jean-Luc Garneau.

A Note on the Poetry of Lucie Thésée

In 1941, his writings banned by the Vichy government and looking for any safe harbor, André Breton found himself in Martinique. Fine weather notwithstanding, he might almost have been at home in Paris: the place was buzzing with Surrealist activity. Aimé Césaire and his circle were just launching *Tropiques*, a literary review dedicated to Surrealism, Négritude, and anti-colonialism. Martiniquean Surrealism was primarily a game for men, despite Suzanne Césaire's theoretical contributions to the journal. But the poetry of an almost completely unknown schoolteacher, Lucie Thésée, appeared in many issues of *Tropiques*, and eventually made its way into the larger Francophone world.

Despite the anthologizing of her work in various collections devoted to writing from the French colonies, and praise from the critic Léon Damas, we still know surprisingly little about Thésée. Certainly this has nothing to do with any shrinking-violet quality on her part: Thésée was a courageous woman, even to the point of recklessness. With Martinique under Vichy rule, *Tropiques* was singled out for persecution. The military government accused the journal of being "racial and sectarian," a vehicle of hatred and division. A letter was sent back to the military officials, saying:

> "Racists," "sectarians," "revolutionaries," "ingrates and traitors to the country," "poisoners of souls," none of these epithets really repulses us. "Poisoners of Souls," like Racine ... "Ingrates and traitors to our good Country," like Zola ... "Revolutionaries," like the Hugo of *Châtiments*. "Sectarians," passionately, like Rimbaud and Lautreamont. Racists, yes. Of the racism of Toussaint Louverture, of Claude McKay and Langston Hughes against that of Drumont and Hitler. As to the rest of it, don't expect for us to plead our case, nor make recriminations, nor hold discussion. We do not speak the same language.

Lucie Thésée's name appears beneath these courageous phrases, next to that of Aimé Césaire.

Sarabande

From a poem by Lucie Thésée.

Look straight, and don't tremble, wreckage of my hanged race:
a sarabande dancer, Japanese muslin tight on her livewire hips,
arrives with the moonlight, fast as the tam-tam drums.
She'll take you to the grand esplanade where the gallows
tell your story, tell of your dim bronze halos
licked away by a pale man's greed.

Leave your gallows tears behind,
the long-drawn vowels of the lost names of flowers,
the long-drawn cries of your burden of grain,
the long-drawn cries of your burden of seed-pods,
and the long-drawn cries of the seed-pods cut and hung.
Shipwreck of my race, twisted in the wind-rush,
fall from your broken gallows, wrack, wreck and driftwood,
my bloodied race.
My bloodied race fearful, scab-dried, sterile, paralyzed,
the low-caste wallflowers trembling at a ball for mice—
no. Leave your gallows, there, those: the gallows of time-gone-by.
Lift your chestnut-dark and heavy limbs, up from out the
    shipwreck's carnage,
and up through those long blue-green rolling waves.
Sing the wind's songs, and collect what's needed, drop by
    shivering drop,
in this, your Lenten fasting, in this, your sorcerer's midnight,
    under this, the whip.
Leave the gallows, the sap of its cut-wood spits on your skin.
You'd hang there, yourself in effigy? No. Live sap runs in the
    driftwood branch.

You'll play, gentle, a light wind in the shimmering green of a
    dancer's beaded muslin skirt,
and your broken music will move in the foolish grass that still
    believes in death—
leave your gallows-bones there, in the fool's green shroud ...
Scratch with the rusted nail of melody, because you live,
    wreckage of my race,
the sky will not forget you, nor the graveyard's earth, fertile and
    walled.
Your blood still dances, a wreckage of joy, joy soured,
obstinate joy, wild and unbroken,
shipwreck of my race, sarabande.

Poem

From a poem by Lucie Thésée.

Handsome, like those foam-topped tidal waves breaking high,
in little crystal globes.
Handsome, like the breeze that lifts a little tuft of tulle. If tulle
were life.
Handsome, like a frozen face, tear-tracked, when the sun
hammers down.
Handsome. Like fire.
Handsome, like the bottomless sky, with that one proud
penetrating star.

But handsome, too, like a sky that's an arching ocean, and an
earth prone as an ocean's floor.
Handsome ocean-sky, and earth-sea floor.
The big question is: where's the man in a scene like this?

Handsome: the man asleep. And the night sky swarms, tropic
and wide.
Handsome, in some ornamental, muggy midnight caught
between cat's paws. Sharp-nailed: they prick.
Handsome: the firefly swarm around you.
Handsome, like a soap bubble grazing a little black dress. Like a
soap-bubble pricked with a pin.
Handsomeness a rainbow, a rainbow an arrow, an arrow in my
chest.
Handsome, like shadows slow-rolling on a Japanese screen.
Handsome motion.
Handsome as life and poison.
Sun-blood handsome. Bleeding sun.

Robert Archambeau

Poem

From a poem by Lucie Thésée.

My head—a set of trash cans, open—gawps:
I am a drain pipe
Gaping wide,
And the blue day funnels through me.
I suck down everything. All of it.
Who doubts my eternity now?
A river, prodigal, roiled with ferocious lives—
You crocodiles, hippopotami—all of it, I suck it down.
Who doubts my eternity now?

My unborn eye.
My coiled and unborn flesh, fetal, without race, without color,
Unborn, when Cupid's little stinging dart
Cut in. The little cynic! My virgin flesh,
Unborn, was marked: dark. A *makanguia*,
Dark with the silky noises of a past
In the darker forests, rich
In a primitive unborn wealth.
Unnumbered. Unnamed. Unborn flesh—red-black:
A sling of plucked rose petals, dying. Vengeance
Was his: my eternity started.
Why not strut in it?

Why not? I'm asking you. Why not me?
Me, my heart-sap thick as a filao-tree's,
Thick with the sap of the impossible
Under green fronds singing in wind.
Me, who skin spikes out filao-tree needles, shivering.

Who said eternity's not mine?

My life doesn't giggle: my life is she
Who kills while laughing.
You, who can't even muster your misery,
You doubt eternity can be mine.
I'll comb my hair with the backbone of the sun.
I'll kiss fire, I'll sail to those ships' holds,
Those crimes on the foam of the waves,
Those crimes between the sea's two horizons:
Liberté, égalité.
Fat-cheeked little beggar in the clouds,
Pale Cupid: I am geysers, craters, belly-of-the-earth.
I throw flame in the flight of my laughter,
I take in everything, drink down song.
I'll shiver and quake with endless flowers blooming.
Eternity, anyway? I'm *Liberté.*

Rapture: The Depths

From a prose poem by Lucie Thésée.

The one-eyed sky: the moon-sky, its light on the tiles of the ruined plantation veranda. And she who comes here often, that black woman, long-boned, slender—long bones stretched on a bed rigged out of scraps and village legends.

Long bones, slight—and chestnut-bronze and unadorned, her skin; her clothes a muslin filigree. Darkness in the dark skirt's folds, her cat mewls for that dead man's face, the moon: Long Bones knows the face it sees.

Long Bones runs long fingers through the cat-fur, forehead first, against the grain, suffers the cat-eyed gaze a while. A brief shrug, a flexion of the neck and shoulders. "He wouldn't take me, he said 'you are afraid,' he lit his cigarette ..."

Darkness in the Dark is not surprised, would suffer her fingers in his fur some more. But Long Bones paces in the light of the one-eyed sky, veranda-length, veranda-length again, to pause, as if to wait for someone, as if to hope. Late, and yet late. If anyone saw, no one would ask: isn't it Long Bones, dark in dark? No one would ask. She comes here often. Day will find her. No one else.

A NOTE ON THE POETRY
OF GABRIEL AND MARCEL PIQUERAY

Gabriel and Marcel Piqueray were identical twins, born in Brussels in 1920. Lovers of jazz and Surrealism, they associated with key figures of the movement, including André Breton and René Magritte (with whom they held regular "Surrealist working meetings" for many years), as well as with the musician Chet Baker and the composer Francis Poulenc. In 1957 they became joint editors of the influential avant-garde journal *Phantomas*, whose contributors included Samuel Beckett, Roland Barthes, René Magritte, Kurt Schwitters, and Jorge Luis Borges, among many others. They published a dozen books (listing "Gabriel and Marcel Piqueray" as authors—the Piqueray brothers did not believe in individual authorship), as well as numerous works in journals, and several works co-authored with Paul Colinet. Gabriel Piqueray died in 1992, Marcel in 1997.

Michel Delville, a sharp-eyed and eclectic critic, has this to say about the milieu in which the Piqueray twins moved:

> *Correspondance*, the first Belgian Surrealist magazine, was founded by Paul Nougé, Camille Goemans and Marcel Lecomte in 1924, the same year as Breton's *First Surrealist Manifesto*. Since that time, Belgian poetry has remained one the European avant-garde's best-kept secrets. The names of Nougé, Chavée and Dumont are conspicuously absent from most anthologies and literary histories, and Belgian Surrealism is generally considered as a non-literary phenomenon and almost systematically confined to the paintings of René Magritte and Paul Delvaux. Unlike many other Belgian writers who moved to Paris to make a career (the examples of Georges Simenon, Henri Michaux, Pierre Alechinsky and many others come to mind) most Belgian Surrealists published their work in their home country, and this may explain their

lack of recognition outside a small circle of connoisseurs and specialists. Perhaps it is the sense of being relegated to the margins of francophone culture that accounts, at least in part, for the radical, convulsive spirit that runs through the history of the Belgian counterculture....

Hierarchy: A Night

From a prose poem by the Piqueray twins.

"Can you see anything?" shouted Danour. He raised the faint and flickering lantern to his face. His squinting features showed his worry.

"I think this road winds on down the mountain," Lora answered.

"Too bad it's so dark tonight. No time to be stuck on the summit, with all this wind—it's not going to be comfortable."

Danour laughed. "To hell with comfort" he said. "The important thing is for us to get down to the valley." The words had hardly left his mouth when he stubbed his toe against a human body. It moved. A voice spoke.

"I don't want to butt in here, but let me tell you this: you'd better not try to go down there." The speaker struggled to sit up, rubbing the sleep from his eyes.

Danour brought his lantern over to have a look at this unexpected dispenser of wisdom. It was a man, about forty, with a big moustache and a bowler hat. As the man stood up he went on explaining: "You see," he said, "at first the summit was covered with lost couples and young families. The brave ones, though, were able to find their way down into the valley. The rest followed. By now they've worked out a system: every family's got its place, packed in side by side from the top on down. You and the missus here will be the final link—you can settle down right here."

"Now, he added, "let me get some sleep. I'm really tired. Good night."

Down in the valley, it sounded like someone got a foot tangled up in the strings of a harp, then became overly apologetic, making careful and elaborate excuses.

Robert Archambeau

What Happens in a Golden Summer

From a prose poem by the Piqueray twins.

The princess passes: a visit to the Hall of Mirrors. The guards are there, smoking their pipes. She takes a pipe from one of them, tastes it: it is unpleasantly bitter. There is blood on the pipe.

The princess passes: a visit to the geometric gardens. Dukes, barons, and marquises loiter by the hedges. The August evening is thick with lilac. Her breast heaves deeply as she takes in the scented air. There is blood on the lilacs.

The princess passes: a visit to the kitchens. There, she finds boards laden with roasted joints, orange peel, pheasant feathers, sage bouquets. The smell of garlic, the scent of burning evergreens, clouds of gnats. Two servants fight behind the princess. Their struggle is fierce and cunning. One of them pulls out his knife, and hurls it at his rival. The blade whirls through the air, missing its goal. The princess is hit, cries out and falls dead, the dagger in her back.

A storm bursts over all of France. There is blood in the King's kitchens.

THE SPROKS

From a series of poems by the Piqueray twins writing under the pseudonym Guy Pezasse, one of their many personae.

Tale of an Experiment

Whenever

He gets a chance

The man

Tears a head of lettuce

Into thousands of pieces

And stuffs them into a very strong

Cup of filtered coffee.
And then
He takes

What remains of the lettuce

And dumps it

Into a vat,

Dripping with coffee.

Robert Archambeau

Example of an Activity

This man's uncle

Sometimes carries

An immense mattress

On his head. And he staggers
With this mattress
From the top of the stairs

To the coal bin,

Where he lays it down
And throws himself on it
Pumping legs in the air
In excitement.

An Action Among Others

The same uncle

Who lives on the seventh floor

In the center of town

Is sometimes

In the habit of filling,
At dawn,
A large pan

With strong black coffee

And balancing it

On the window sill

With the help of his nephew;
Then sending it
Careening into the street,
Not giving a fuck
About it.

Robert Archambeau

Tale of Another Action

It is this same gentleman

Who, with the help of his uncle,
Fills an immense cast-iron
Stove

With gooseberry jam.
When they've done this,
The gentleman and his uncle

Throw handfuls of jelly
At each other's faces
For fun.

An Activity Among Others

What also happens

Sometimes,

Is that the gentleman, his uncle
And his nephew

Tear many heads
Of lettuce into thousands of pieces
Then pour strong coffee
On them,

In a vacant lot
On a slope,
With
Coal heaps

And piles of shattered windowpanes

At the bottom of
The slope.
Then
They speed down the slope

On their bicycles

Without braking,

Their legs spread wide,

Feet held away from
The pedals;
And then,
At the bottom of this slope,

The tires make a crackling noise

In the coal

And a farting noise

In the shattered
Windowpanes. Then
The gentleman,
His uncle

And his nephew

Jump off

Their bikes

And pelt each other

With old heads of lettuce,
Very strong coffee,
Coal,

And shattered windowpanes
Until they take up shovels
While leaping
On mattresses

Filled with plaster
And pumping
Their legs in the air
In the gooseberry jelly

Of their excitement.

Robert Archambeau

A Pedal-Pusher Said to Me

From a poem by the Piqueray twins.

A pedal-pusher said to me
No braykaiser
No sterfput
A-stepping and a-stoumping cretin-wise
Could drive a man to madness
Just as no thousand Orphas all draped in damp peignoirs
Doing their great kochera
With the prima donna
Of Iquzegdamoda
Of Paczevast
Of Anunec
Each Orpha in an evening gown
Imploring of our pedal-pusher
To go a-step and go a-stoump all over yet again
With a thousand mops
And a thousand sterfputs imploring them
The braykaiser in me
The sterfput in me
The mop in me
The kochera in me
The Paczevast in me
The Anunec in me
The Iquzegdamoda in me
And all the stoumpers
The steppers
The mops
The evening gowns
And all the Orphas

All the pedal-pushers
The damp peignoirs
The cretins
The prima donnas
Who beg
The kocheras
The Iquzegdamodas
The Anunecs
And all the Paczevasts
To step
And to stoump for the sake of love
The great flowering love
Of a thousand pedal-pushers
A-draped in damp peignoirs
Will lead no braykaiser
No sterfput
No mop
No kochera
No Paczevast
No Anunec
No Iquzegdamoda
To implore a man to madness
And that is what a-stepping and a-stoumping cretin-wise
A pedal-pusher said to me

V

AFTERWORD

HATING THE OTHER KIND OF POETRY

1. This is not a how-to guide

It isn't quite a how-not-to guide either, but I suppose that's closer.

2. "What you *should* be doing," or: the limits of disinterest

A few years ago, when the Conceptualist poet Kenneth Goldsmith was making big waves in the little demitasse cup of the American poetry world, I wrote an essay that tried to explain what his work had to offer and what it didn't. The email I received in response was gratifying in quantity, if bewildering in content. I'd tried merely to describe Goldsmith's work, but I found I was condemned for having praised him, praised for having condemned him, praised for having praised him, and condemned for having condemned him—all in roughly equal measure. The uniform distribution of responses on the chart of praise and blame gave me some reassurance that my attempt at mere description hadn't unintentionally become a clear act of advocacy or disapproval, but it also confirmed my suspicion that people were not particularly inclined to view as innocent an essay that did its best to remain neutral: an agenda, the thinking went, must lurk just below the surface. I am not so naïve as to believe that truly disinterested inquiry is possible, but the notion that we may approach disinterest asymptotically—like a curving line that comes ever closer to another line without actually touching it—was clearly alien to a literary audience that had been through several decades of the hermeneutics of suspicion. Only M, a critic from whom I had learned a great deal over the years, and who had always been kind to me, saw the essay for what it was, or tried to be—and she didn't like it. "What you *should* be doing," she told me, "is making a strong case for the poetry you believe in, and against the poetry you don't." She'd been doing exactly that for decades, and I knew people who revered her for it. I also knew people who all but spat when they said her name.

3. "That never works," or: pluralism and failure

It wasn't the first time I'd been told something like that. Back in the final decade of the last century, when I was starting up a little magazine devoted to poetry, I received much helpful advice from K, a poet and critic who, like M, had long championed the more experimental wing of poetry. I was young and dewy-eyed, and had the usual delusions about what a little magazine might accomplish. "What I really want to do," I said, over coffee in some dingy university café, "is make a space for different kinds of poets to come together and talk to one another." "Yeah," said K, my senior by a decade and a grizzled veteran of the long march of experimental poetry from the wilderness into the academy, "that never works."

Years later, long after the fate of my magazine had proved K right, I was in touch with him again, this time after the early death of another poet, a tremendously charming American who'd moved to London and written formal verse in traditional rhyme and meter. He and K had been friends in their grad school days—"dope smoking buddies, mostly," as K put it—but had, despite a few joyous reunions when all arguments were put aside, fallen out over poetry. They hadn't seen each other in years, and the news of the poet's death hit K hard. "I always thought there'd come a time when all these poetry wars would be behind us, and we'd be friends again" he told me. I didn't know what to say.

4. "I find your paper irritating," or: looking at the back of your own head

I don't remember what I said, and that's not what's important anyway: what's important is the aftermath. I was standing rather smugly before an audience at an academic conference where I'd just delivered a paper on a poet of some repute, fielding questions along with the other panelists, when I saw the formidable white mane of C rise above the crowd. A scholar whose elegant suits and forceful manner gave him an aura closer to that of a Mafioso than one would have thought possible for a professor of literature, C did not look happy, and he was looking at me. "I find your paper irritating," he said. "Don't misunderstand: I liked the other papers more, but didn't find them interesting enough to be irritating. Come to think of it, I didn't find your paper interesting either—it's the nature of my irritation with it that's interesting."

In the well-crafted spoken paragraphs that followed, C took my paper apart, but he did much more than that: he also disassembled his own reaction to my paper, pulled out the assumptions behind that reaction, held them up to the sunlight and saw what was beautiful and meaningful in those assumptions, and what was narrow and even cruel. It was magnificent. With the possible exception of the time an esteemed English editor took a cricket bat to some of my prose and beat it into a wet pulp from which he then formed a proper essay, C's takedown of my paper remains my favorite literary chastening. It also showed me something one could do with a text that wasn't advocacy (it was about as far from advocacy of what I'd said as one could get) and wasn't simply condemnation either. Nor was it disinterested or neutral explanation, of the sort I'd tried to supply in my essay on Goldsmith, and it certainly wasn't any sort of pluralistic live-and-let-live move, either. In the encounter with an irritating text, C had taken a step back and seen not only the irksome text in front of him, but seen himself looking at it. It was as if he stood behind himself, looking at the back of his own head. *Ekstasis*, the ancient Greeks called it—standing outside oneself. It was C's interpretive ecstasy, and we watched in wonder.

5. "That fucking Merwin," or: the back of Creeley's head

I know a lot of people who loved Robert Creeley, who saw the old sage of Black Mountain and Buffalo as a generous mentor and friend, and he certainly was that. He may turn out to have meant more to more younger poets than any other figure of his generation. But if you read his letters, you see that he had as large a capacity for hatred as he had for paternal or avuncular love. He despises Theodore Roethke and Louis Simpson, hurls abuse at Helen Vendler, spews bile in the direction of Louise Glück and Charles Wright, dismisses Kenneth Koch as a lightweight, and talks about cutting Frank O'Hara (the editors of the letters work hard, in a footnote, to explain this away as metaphorical, and may be right). "Fuck him," he says of Kenneth Patchen, and he tells us how "that fucking Merwin" is a "a symbol of rot." He clearly sees battle lines drawn between a kind of poetry he admires and the kinds he does not, and he takes exception when the people who should be on his side appear to cross the line and embrace the enemy. "I will never forget this," he writes to Kenneth Rexroth, when the older poet treasonously supported Roethke; and when William Carlos Williams spoke approvingly of W.H. Auden, Creeley demanded to know whether someone had held a gun to Williams' back. Academics have a special place in Creeley's inferno—even after so many of them had come to accept his views about who the important poets were. In 1985, he tells us that academics wouldn't deign to write about Williams or Olson—and does so with such vehemence that I wouldn't want to have been the one to tell him of the half dozen prominent academic articles on Olson that year alone, or the three dozen on Williams, or of the professor who'd just edited the sixth volume of Creeley's correspondence with Olson. Resentment outlives its occasion, and those who harbor it don't want to be reminded of the fact.

When I've mentioned this vituperative side of Creeley to

his old friends and allies, they've been quick to point out that Creeley and the poets he supported were for a long time—and in some quarters are even now—the subject of a disdain every bit as strong as that which we find in Creeley's letters. They're not wrong, these friends of Creeley. You won't find as much invective about Creeley and his peers in the letters of those about whom he snarled, except perhaps in recent years, but that's simply because silence is the snarling of the powerful.

What, I wonder, would Creeley have seen if he'd looked, not at those he despised, but at himself looking at them? What if, like C, he had seen himself from outside himself? I suppose he'd have seen a man in something like the condition Pierre Bourdieu describes when he discusses what happens to an art when it is no longer playing for stakes beyond art itself in any meaningful way—when there are few significant financial, political, or ecclesiastical rewards at stake, when it operates at the margins of money and power. Under these conditions, it is the practitioners of the art itself who hand out the rewards, and while those rewards may be in some minimal sense matters of money or power or hierarchical position, they are primarily matters of recognition. No one's been made a lord for poetry since Tennyson, and no one hoping for riches nowadays would present a poem to a head of state, as Edmund Spenser did—successfully—to Elizabeth I. Bourdieu tells us that when the practitioners of an art become the primary decision makers about who gets the (largely symbolic) rewards, we see a phenomenon called "the social aging of art." This is a process in which one group—generally marginal, young, or both—seeks to discredit those who practice the art differently. One doesn't compete for money in a commercial market, but for prestige in a symbolic market, and the way to do that isn't to woo customers, but to discredit the other guys. It's no accident that the proliferation of manifestos and aesthetic dogmas came about at the moment when complex developments in mass education, publishing, and communications rendered poetry unviable as a market commodity. Freed from external demands—another way of saying "left to fend for themselves"—the poets proliferated styles and frequently looked with disdain at those whose work took a different path than their own. "That fucking Merwin," one might utter of another.

6. Conquistadors and anthropologists

The Polish philosopher Leszek Kołakowski once wrote with apparent sympathy of a group of people who believed fervently in their own ideals and disdained those of others, saying:

> A few years ago I visited the pre-Columbian monuments in Mexico and was lucky enough, while there, to find myself in the company of a well known Mexican writer, thoroughly versed in the history of the Indian peoples of the region. Often in the course of explaining to me the significance of many things I would not have understood without him, he stressed the barbarity of the Spanish soldiers who had ground the Aztec statues into dust and melted down the exquisite gold figurines to strike with the image of the Emperor. I said to him, 'you think these people were barbarians; but were they not, perhaps, true Europeans, indeed the last true Europeans? They took their Christian and Latin civilization seriously; and it is because they took it seriously that they saw no reason to safeguard pagan idols; or to bring the curiosity and aesthetic detachment of archeologists into their consideration of things imbued with a different, and therefore hostile religious significance. If we are outraged at their behavior it is because we are indifferent, both to their civilization, and to our own.'

Kołakowski was, however, playing devil's advocate—since, for him, the better angels of European civilization were not the conquistadors, but the anthropologists. "The anthropologist," Kołakowski writes, must suspend his own norms, his judgments, his mental, moral, and aesthetic habits in order to penetrate as far as possible into the viewpoint of another and assimilate his way of perceiving the world. And even though no one, perhaps, would claim to have achieved total success in this effort, even though total success would presuppose an epistemological impossibility—to enter entirely into the mind of the object of inquiry while maintaining the distance and objectivity of the scientist—the effort is not in vain. We cannot completely achieve the position of an observer seeing himself from the outside, but we may do so partially.

Like the scholar C after he heard my irritating paper at the conference years ago, when confronted with that which is alien to our sensibilities we may make the attempt to stand outside ourselves, and in doing so see something other than an object of disdain. Indeed, we may get a kind of doubled or even tripled vision: we'll know the thing we're looking at—a poem, say—on something like it's own terms, as well as on ours. Moreover, we might discover something about our own assumptions—our assumptions and, one hopes, ourselves.

7. The potter's wheel and the back of my own head

When I wrote "one hopes" in the previous sentence, I suppose what I really meant was "I hope." But why hope for this kind of approach to poetry, as opposed to the naked partisanship of M or of K? Perhaps the explanation is generational: both M and K are older than I am, and I'm deeper into middle age than I care to admit. The names I recognized among those who wrote to praise or blame me for my article on Goldsmith belonged to an older set, too.

Perhaps as the memory of the exclusion of one sort of poet from the privileged world of academe becomes less a living thing, and more a matter of history, the rhetoric of partisanship will fade. Creeley could still feel marginal even after he was a

Chancellor of the Academy of American Poets and a leading figure in the best-funded poetry program in the country, but that was because his formative experiences were those of a truly marginalized outcast. Nowadays, when I read screeds against the Poetry Foundation by full professors at top MFA programs, I suspect what I'm seeing are the last embers of the old fires of outsider resentment. The revolution of the young against the old and the new against the outmoded described by Pierre Bourdieu—the revolution that launched a thousand manifestoes and set anthologists at one another's throats—was the product of a climate of resource scarcity. When there were virtually no external rewards for poets, or when the few rewards (steady teaching jobs, say) were monopolized by a single group (let's call them the poets associated with the New Criticism), partisanship could rage, resentments flare, and those who wrote poetry different from one's own could very easily be cursed as lightweights and symbols of rot. But when academe has long since made room for poets as diverse as Rae Armantrout, Billy Collins, Claudia Rankine, and Kenneth Goldsmith, it's harder to rage convincingly against a monolithic establishment. At least it is for the moment: perhaps the crumbling of the academic humanities will give us a renewed outbreak of heartfelt resentment.

Maybe, though, it's not generational: maybe it's just me. When I ask myself why I resist M's injunction to fight for the kind of poetry I find appealing, and against those kinds to which I am not immediately drawn, the first thing I think of is not my generation, or those coming after me. The first thing I think of is my father, bent over his potter's wheel. Dad is a ceramic artist, and I spent my pre-teen years as an art-school brat of the 1970s—or, to be more precise, as a *provincial* art-school brat of the 1970s, Dad being a professor at the deeply rusticated University of Manitoba. What this means is simple:

I saw a lot of abstract painters, earthwork sculptors, conceptual artists, installation artists, photorealists and post-minimalists jockeying around for fame and position, hoping like hell to get themselves off the Canadian prairies and back to the American east coast or at the very least to L.A., the kind of cultural centers from whence they'd come. My father had made the opposite move, leaving the faculty of the prestigious Rhode Island School of Design for the boondocks, in part because, like all ceramic artists (and unlike those post-minimalists and conceptualists), he harbored no illusions about becoming any kind of art star. Outside of Japan and a few other Asian cultures, there's simply no prestige to pottery, and no amount of raging or resentment will change that. Creeley could go from the outside in, railing at his enemies all the way, but there's a notable lack of revolutionary rhetoric among ceramicists, who experience the climate of non-recognition as a permanent condition, not as an injustice to be combatted. Most of our attitudes are absorbed from our environment without much conscious reflection on our part, and I imagine my distaste for battles about aesthetic recognition and campaigns against forms of art different from one's own comes less from all those grad school hours reading Bourdieu and Adorno than from seeing my dad roll his eyes at the rhetoric and ambitious yearnings of his colleagues.

Whether the resistance to partisan polemic is a matter of generational and institutional change, or simply a matter of my own peculiar formation, I don't know. I do know that my own resistance to polemic is strong enough that I don't even want this essay to be an advocacy of one approach to poetry over another, although at some level I suppose it inevitably is. What I want this essay to be is less a program than an examination— an attempt to look directly (and impossibly) at the back of my own head.

8. These poems

These poems—so often riffs on, remixes of, replies to, or deeply unfaithful translations of what others have written—are mostly attempts to enter sensibilities other than my own, and to step back and look at the results of those entrances. They are what I see when I look (impossibly) at the back of my own head.

ABOUT THE AUTHOR

Robert Archambeau was born in Providence, Rhode Island in 1968, but his family moved to Canada before his first birthday—a strange kind of homecoming, given that his ancestors were among the first settlers of Quebec. Never quite at home as a Canadian or American, he came to inhabit what he describes as "the world's least interesting trans-national identity." He has vivid memories of his parents, at the end of the Nixon administration, considering putting an "America: Love It or Leave It" bumper sticker on their car, next to the Canadian license plate. He attended the University of Manitoba, where his father, a ceramic artist, taught, and where he had a fraught relationship with the regionalist poetic movement then in fashion among the poets associated with the university. Later, looking for a poetry that was concerned with regional identity but that was also attracted to the remote, the arcane, and the displaced, he discovered the work of the American poet John Matthias, whose work and background were as English as they were American.

Archambeau went to study under Matthias at the University of Notre Dame, where he wrote a doctoral dissertation on the appropriation of Wordsworth's regionalist poetics by postcolonial writers, and where he accidentally blundered into an M.F.A. by hanging out in Matthias' living room, where the writing seminars were conducted, and writing poems.

A few regionalist poems made it into Archambeau's first collection of poems, *Home and Variations*, but what really came to fascinate him, as both poet and critic, were acts of creative appropriation and re-imagination. His chapbook *Citation Suite* consisted of a long poem composed only of quotations from various sources spliced into one another until they created a language of their own, and this pointed him in a direction his work was to follow. The present book and the chapbook *Slight Return: Remix and Ekphrasis* contain writing in this mode: an inhabiting and reworking of found text, generally literary in nature.

As a critic, Archambeau has been increasingly drawn to questions of the social position of poetry, of how it has functioned in different contexts. His first critical book, *Laureates and Heretics: Six Careers in American Poetry*, examined the reputations and career paths of six poets who studied at Stanford in the 1960s—including two, Robert Pinsky and Robert Hass, who went on to serve as poets laureate of the United States—with an eye toward understanding the intersection of aesthetic choices and poetic renown. A later study, *The Poet Resigns: Poetry in a Difficult World*, examines the question of the kinds of social conditions that make poetry popular or marginal. He has also edited several books, including *Word Play Place: Essays on the Poetry of John Matthias* and *Letters of Blood and Other English Writings of Göran Printz-Påhson*. He taught for a time at Lund University in Sweden and is now professor of English at Lake Forest College, where he teaches Romanticism, literary theory and, occasionally, creative writing.

OTHER BOOKS BY ROBERT ARCHAMBEAU

The Poet Resigns: Poetry in a Difficult World

Laureates and Heretics: Six Careers in American Poetry

Home and Variations: Poems

As editor:

Letters of Blood and Other English Works of Göran Printz-Påhlson

The &NOW Awards: The Best Innovative Writing

Word Play Place: Essays on the Poetry of John Matthias

www.ingramcontent.com/pod-product-compliance
Lightning Source LLC
Chambersburg PA
CBHW032105080426
42733CB00006B/425